The MAN-ual:

The Single Mother's Guide to

Dating and Moving On

By: Bernard Green Jr.

Copyright

Printed in the United States of America

First Printing, 2016

ISBN 978-0-692-65356-2

Books may be purchased by contacting the
publisher and author at:
Itswrittenpublishing@gmail.com

Published by: Its Written Publishing LLC
Smyrna, GA

Acknowledgments

Many thanks to:

Everyone who supported me.

My friends; Johnny Green, Wallace Brown, Michael Lee, Eugene Burns, Winston Reddick, Adrianne George

My Editor's: Mike Valentino and Keina Jackson

Cover Illustrator: Nikka Green

Special Thanks My Parents Karen Thomas and Bernard Green Sr.

My girlfriend Sierra Henry, You did all the dirty work in this whole exhausting process and I thank you for all your support babe.

Last but not least I want to thank all the single mothers out here, keep ya' head up because without ya'll it would be no us. Thank you ladies and God Bless.

Table of Contents

Author's Note

I feel at this stage of my dating life I meet a lot of
women who either have a child or children. Now
the kids are definitely not the problem at all, the
problem is you ladies. Now before you start getting
defensive let me explain. How many times have you
ladies either had a good man or passed over a good
man because of your situation with the father of
your child? I understand you created a life with this
man, but any man can create a life. So many times, I
see women missing out on their happy ending
because they can't get over their nightmare. Well
I'm here to help. I'm going to touch a lot of topics
from my personal experiences and I want to share

them with you all, so that you can find your happy ending.

I used to be the guy who said, "I wouldn't date a woman with kids." or say things like, "I don't want a ready-made family." As I got older, I realized that's not what I really meant. I believe what was preventing me from dating a woman with children was the fact that, in the back of my mind, I always felt like I could never compete with the father of your child because you had something that we didn't have, your child. So I always felt I was walking on eggshells. I believed that at any moment she could go back to him. I always thought that if I had a child with her, maybe her child's father and I would be viewed as equal. Only then, could she love me and care about me as much as she did him. So I want to take the time to apologize to all the women with children out there, especially my ex, who I did so wrong because of my selfishness. All she wanted me to do was step up and be a father figure for that beautiful little girl and I couldn't do it. I lost a good woman because of my selfish, foolish, and childish ways. It's a tough pill to swallow but I had to get over it. I didn't realize it at the time but now I know and I want to help. I hope you all enjoy.

Women often use the infamous term "this is my child" and those words, more often than not, can cause a disconnect between her and the new boyfriend or husband, as well as between him and the child. My mother was notorious for that. I never respected the new man in her life because I always knew I really didn't have to listen and only respect him enough to not get in trouble.

At the same time, the man must know and respect his boundaries when it comes to disciplining the child. He has to understand his role, especially if that child already has a father in his or her life. That's why it's important for your new man and the child's father to have open communication. Both of them can prevent some lines from being crossed. To be honest with you, if I had a child I don't think I would want another man disciplining my son or daughter, especially not whooping them. I think grounding them is acceptable, taking into account the complexity of the relationship but again communication is key. I'll touch base more on that subject in the upcoming chapters.

Chapter 1

Know When to Introduce Your Child to a New Partner

Ladies, ladies, ladies it's important to know when it's appropriate to introduce little man man or little Kylie to your new partner. The worst and most uncomfortable situation in the world is being invited over to a woman's house for an evening of "Netflix and Chill" and as soon as he or she walks through the door, you're being bombarded by your overly excited son or daughter.

Example, I was invited over by a young lady one night. The first thing that comes to my mind is ok, it's 'bout to go down. I grab a bottle of wine, some popcorn and start my free 30 day membership. I get to the house and she's cooking, everything is going smoothly and then, out of nowhere, her son runs out from the back of the house screaming and hollering. Now mind you, I don't have anything against kids, I love them and can't wait to have one, but this is not a good look if this is our first time spending an evening in the house together. The night of passion and popcorn turned into a night of babysitting and me pretending that I liked this bad ass little boy while wondering where the hell is his daddy at? I know, I know, you guys are a package deal or whatever -- we understand this -- but all I am saying is give us some time to get to know each other first. That way it's a lot easier for us to accept your child or else it's going to be fake and forced.

I can remember this other time when this chick called me and announced, "Me and my kids comin' over." I'm thinking, *wait... what?* How can you tell a woman that the way my house is set up, it's not set up for two little boys to be running around getting into my stuff tearing up my massage chair and putting his little dirty hands on my flat screen? And since you don't really know the kids you can't say, "Aye, boy, sit yo butt down somewhere!" While at the same time trying not to step on anyone's toes. It's just a very delicate situation that has to be handled in a very calculated manner because at this stage of you guys' relationship it's just pure attraction; I didn't even know if I liked her. I'm almost certain she's not my type, which is another reason you ladies have to be careful when introducing your kids to a man because he may only 'wanna hit' just like I did.

Also, ladies, miss me with the 'gotta find a babysitter lie' because when I met you at the club you had a babysitter then so what's the difference from then to now. Every time I want to hang out you have to find a babysitter. What the hell! Believe me if a man likes you he will start asking about your kids or wanting to start hanging out with you and them. A man will start doing things like taking lil' man to the barbershop with him, spending time with him, and even babysit while you're at work, but you can't force it. You have to let it happen naturally.

Chapter 2

Communication with the Child's Father Should Be About The Child, That is It!

Ladies, there is no reason for you and him to be constantly working on your so-called friendship. You do not have to be friends just because you share a child together, you do your job and let him do his job. Too many times you see a good girl who ends up hurt because she constantly keeps falling for a man who barely takes care of his own child. Ladies, one thing about us, we will do anything to keep you and most importantly to keep hittin' that, so if that means using the child as leverage by constantly telling you that you guys are going to be a family then so be it. Stop falling for the lies! Stop telling yourself "he will get it right one day" because if his own kid isn't enough for that to happen then what is? Just because you have a child together doesn't mean you or him are obligated to be together, be good co-parents and stop being controlled by the title of "baby daddy." I'm tired of the, "I'm trying to make it work for the sake of the children," excuse. Hear me out, that's all fine and dandy, you want your family back and I understand -- but if the brotha has kids with other women and he still has an ongoing relationship with his other baby mothers then what the hell makes you think those women aren't thinking the same way you are. Let that marinate on you for a minute.

When he drops his child off there is no reason he should step foot in your home. Before you know it one thing leads to another and now he's in the bed and you're thinking he still wants to be with you. Ladies, you have to break that cycle of sleeping with the father of your child. It just creates confusion between the two of you and then when you see him on IG with his boo you want to get mad and be spiteful by doing things like arguing with the other woman or worse keeping him away from his child. I want to ask you beautiful ladies a question: if you're dating a man and you know he has children he barely takes care of, he doesn't talk about his kids and you've never seen pictures or anything indicating he has kids, why in the hell would you go and get pregnant by the deadbeat your damn self? I asked a woman in a similar situation and she gives me some silly excuse like you can't judge someone on their past and that things are going to be different now. Ladies, please don't tell me you all think this way, this logic is a horrible way of thinking. Let me tell you something, once a deadbeat always a deadbeat. What makes you so different from the previous woman he had his first child with? Ask yourself that question. I know a lot of guys try to blame the woman for him not seeing his kids but believe me if a man wants to see his kids he will do everything in his power to do so. Stop trying to turn a deadbeat into hubby because he is not. Start looking for father figures for your children and not the freshest dude in the club with the biggest muscles and oh and by the way, some of your "Man Crush Mondays" look like horrible father figures

Chapter 3

Your Baby Father's New Girlfriend is Not the Enemy

Let me be clear about this, just because your child's father has moved on and is happy somewhere else does not make him any less of a father, it just means he found love somewhere else. Furthermore, you should not be harassing this woman and making Facebook statuses about her. It's not her fault you keep falling for the same lies and now you're mad because you feel used and led on. What beef could you possibly have about a woman you don't even know? How is arguing with her and calling her phone going to help with co-parenting? The way social media is used to bully and start trouble is ridiculous. You guys have to be adults about the situation because if he is serious about her then she will be around your child and there is nothing you can do about it. She also has to know her role and understand that child is a part of the relationship as well. Take the time to get to know her. Discuss the way you guys can communicate about the child and more importantly have a cordial relationship for the child's sake. I am so tired of hearing stuff like, "You bet not have that bitch around my child" or "I'm not letting my kids come over until you get rid of the bitch." Come on, ladies, how is this type of behavior accomplishing anything? I know this may not be the best example but take Lil Wayne for instance, all of his baby mothers get along, which allows the kids to be around their siblings as well. Whether Lil Wayne is there or not the moms still communicate with each other. They are not cattie and they don't make it where it's a competition between the kids for their father's love and attention. So with that being said, if you guys are no longer dating, who he is dating is not your concern. Your only concern is the child. As long as the new woman treats your kid or kids well you should have no problem with her. Look at her as another babysitter for you when you want to go out or something. It takes a village to raise children why not come together and make life easier for yourselves.

Chapter 4

Your Child's Father's Other Children

One thing that used to irk me growing up was when my mother used to use the word half-brother. There is no such thing as half in a child's eyes. Whether that other child comes from the mother or father, he or she is their full brother or sister- PERIOD. I don't know who made that term up about only being half related to your siblings through the father but it's dumb and let's end it in this book right now.

Now back to business. If your child's father has other kids, it is important for those kids to establish a relationship because family is important. Many times your child's father has other children outside of your relationship which is good because it prevents your child from being the only child, which isn't much fun for a kid. Kids want siblings. It lets them know they are not alone out here. Even if your child's father is not involved in your kid's life make an effort to keep the kids in contact with their siblings. Especially when you ladies decide you're done having kids after your first one and that's mainly because your child's father wasn't shit- but you chose him.

That's another issue that bothers me, not trying to get off subject or anything but this has to be said. When I meet a woman with kids and she goes, "I'm not having any more kids," do you think that is fair to someone who doesn't have any already? Why are you punishing him because the first guy you decided to have a kid with didn't go well? Not saying that your kid can't be his but every man wants to make at least one of his own. I know me, personally, I would love to make a Bernard Green III AKA "lil trey" but if you're not willing to even consider creating another life with the new guy then maybe you need to find someone who is ok with you not wanting to have any more kids or already has kids. Just make sure that when you do meet that guy he treats your kids and his kids equally, no favoritism between them. A lot of times men and women subconsciously do that, so be mindful of those things because the children are innocent. I know it's a hard thing to do but kids can sense that stuff. Make sure you reiterate that to your families as well, make sure they know to treat the step kids as family. I remember feeling left out around holiday seasons at my dad's house when we would go over his wife's family house and everyone would be exchanging gifts and I wouldn't get anything from her side of the family and if I did it was some ugly shirt from Walmart. I'm only telling you ladies this because stuff like that can make kids feel as if they are not a part of that family when in fact they are. It's just up to you to make sure stuff like that doesn't happen.

Chapter 5

Child Support!

This might be one of the most sensitive chapters in this manual. But I would like to ask some of you a question. When you made your child or children, did you make that child alone, was it like what happened when Mary had Jesus? No, I thought so, so why is it so hard for some of you to put these men on child support? I mean it's in the title, say it with me CH-IL-D SU-PP-ORT. Oh and to the ladies who say he buys my child anything he or she wants, let's just remember all kids want are Jays, toys and games; that's not what support is. Support is help keeping a roof over your child's head, help with that car note and gas when you pick them up from school because you're the one waking up every day at six in the morning getting the kids dressed and ready for school. You're the one up all night giving them medicine and caring for them when they have a fever. You didn't make that child alone, so he should help to raise that child too.

Here's where I think the problem lies, many women aren't thinking rationally but emotionally when interacting with an absentee father. Some of the famous quotes I hear when I ask the question about child support are: "I don't need a man for shit, my child don't want for nothing; I don't need a man, if he don't wanna help that's fine me and my child don't want for nothing;" and lastly some of them are just flat out scared to put him on child support for the simple fact that you might lose him his attention. I don't understand why you would want to be with someone who you have to beg to help out with you both share. Oh and I almost forgot this famous saying by some of you ladies, "I shouldn't have to make him do anything, he should want to help." Ladies, let me tell you something, some men don't even like to pay their own bills but they pay them anyway. Right? Think of child support like that, if he doesn't pay for his kids, just like anything else in life, there will be consequences. In a man's case that's jail which I think is perfectly acceptable for a deadbeat father. Why should you have to handle all that responsibility alone and he runs the street in his new car and new clothes without a care in the world. You didn't make the child alone so why should you have to raise a child alone. If he's not going to

spend some time with his kids, the least he could do

is spend the check. Hey, who knows maybe once he

starts paying for his child he never sees maybe he

will start wanting to see where all his money is

going and start spending time with his kid.

Chapter 6

Stop Playing Family

Ladies, stop allowing him to have his cake and eat it too. Too many times I see women allowing the child's father to play both sides. What I mean by play both sides is allowing him to come in and out of your life while he has a whole other relationship going on. Those late night "I love you texts" or those once a month relations you guys engage in has to stop. How do you plan on finding your happy ending if you keep going back to your nightmare? I heard a guy tell a woman the other day that she better not have another man around his kids. I was like is this dude serious? I'm around your child more than you! Some of you are dumb enough to listen to that nonsense. What makes him think he can have a say regarding who you bring around your kids when he's barely around? My thing is why would a woman want a man who is not willing to be there for your kids? Hell, he's not! I mean, ladies, you have to stop being controlled by that title of "the baby daddy" because you never know what you're missing out on chasing this dude who just won't do right.

However, watch who you bring around them, too. Another reason I didn't like dating women with kids was because I knew I was only talking to her for one thing and meeting the child would be awkward knowing that all I wanted to do was sleep with her. Not all men have remorse like me, I know some guys who don't care. Some will even use your kid as a pawn just to get closer to you and get what they want. Also, be aware of the men who only care about you and not about your child, you can tell this by their actions when he never wants to include your child in activities like you don't even have a kid. I am guilty of this unfortunately. I couldn't stand when she would say let's all go to some carnival or circus because I always felt as if I was playing family. I remember this one time I bought some tickets to the universal soul circus for my ex's daughter. So on the way out a lot of the little girls were sitting on their father's necks, her daughter asked me if she could sit on my neck and because of my old selfish reasons I told a five-year old no. That's one of the things I regret because I was taking my own selfishness out on an innocent child. Watch out for the snakes in the grass, ladies, they are very deceitful, I know because I was one of them and I regret that to this day.

Chapter 7

Tax Season Tyrone

Ladies, stop letting your baby daddies come around during tax season please! I call these types of guys "tax season Tyrones". This is how this situation works, ladies, you work hard all year, working and raising your kids, 365 days out the year for you and your family. Not your boyfriend, not your baby daddy, not your side piece, for you! Do not let your baby daddy come in your life and ask to claim a child on his taxes and he hasn't called your child and wished him happy birthday, Merry Christmas, Happy New Year, hell he won't even buy the kids a bag of a candy on Halloween but he wants to claim the kids on his taxes. Smarten up, ladies, all he does with that money is take it to the strip club and spend it on Peaches and Coco from Blue Flame. Where was he when man man was sick or when Kylie needed money for cheerleading uniforms? It's just so crazy how over the past few weekends I have been noticing a lot of happy couples floating through the malls and the jewelry stores lately lookin' all happy. But before you go and buy Tyrone the new chain he asked for, just ask yourself, where was he two months ago when you were asking him for money for the kids or help with some bills? I'm not opposed to you helping your man or your child's father get on their feet, just make sure you look at his actions before you cash out on your man, your "bae," or whatever he is to you. Oh and by the way, helping them to get on their feet doesn't mean go buy them some pounds so they can flip. Half the time that ends up being a big waste of time, money and even worse, jail time. I just hate seeing women being taken advantage of like that. I was talking to this one woman and her car's transmission went out a few weeks ago. So as you can guess she is having all kinds of problems getting back and forth to work. So I asked her, "Well, didn't you just get your taxes?"

She replied, "Yeah, me and Mike went to Miami."

Mike is a "tax season Tyrone," he has no place to live and no car but he stays fly. Now Mike has been dating her for one month, somehow this Tyrone talked her into going to Miami and spending all her refund, so now she's back to square one: no car and struggling getting rides back and forth. All I could do is shake my head. You gotta do better, ladies, she is not the only victim of Tax Season

Tyrone. I know some of you probably are with him

right now, just getting back from some fancy

restaurant you just picked up the tab for, while he

was snap chatting videos of the meal you paid for.

Stay woke ladies and be aware of the Tax Season

Tyrone's.

Chapter 8

Watch Who You Bring Around Your Children

Do a background check on your man before you invite that dude who's been locked up for the last three years into your home, or the dude with three kids who you have never seen once since you guys have been dating. A lot of these dudes couldn't care less about your kids and some of them are only using you just for a place to live. Some of you are so desperate for a man you don't even care. You done moved this complete stranger in, now your house is the new trap spot and you're his trap queen while the kids lay their heads there. I told my friend the other day about this woman I have a lot of love for, she has three kids and the only men I see her attracted to are drug dealers, rappers and credit card scammers. When she shows me some of the dudes she is interested in I always tell her the dudes she likes look like horrible father figures. She always gets mad and curses me out saying stuff like, "I'm not looking for all that." Really, well what the hell are you looking for in a man? Now she doesn't bring anyone around her children, but I think the reasoning behind that goes back to my point about those men not being good for her and the children.

At what point do you stop dating a certain type of man only for yourself and find men who would make great examples for your children? Think about your kids. I'm starting to read too many articles about men molesting or abusing children. It hurts my heart when I see things like that because I just feel like sometimes this stuff can be avoided. You shouldn't be leaving these men you have known for a month alone with your kids, talking about "he's good with my kids." Sweetheart, I bet he is. I'm just speaking the truth because someone has to say it. Now I'm not blaming you ladies because there really are some sickos out here but you have to do a better job of screening these men.

Ladies, please stop doing drugs in front of your children. Stop smoking weed and smoking cigarettes, doing coke, or whatever it is you do. Kids are very impressionable and eventually, A. they are either going to resent you for your bad habits or B, pick up those bad habits themselves.

The other day I saw a lesbian couple and one of the chicks was holding a baby. The baby had to be no more than a month old and the other woman was just smoking the cigarette like there was no baby around. That's just a blatant sign of disrespect to me. I swear if I had a kid and I found out the mother of my child's new boyfriend or girlfriend was disrespecting my kids like that, there would be hell to pay! Ladies, you have to let that man or woman know that your kids come first and have respect for your kids. If he loves you he better love those kids.

Earlier I talked about knowing when to introduce your child, well this isn't only for our sake but your kids' sake as well. Ladies, be careful when you meet a man and you have a child with him. Sometimes men tend to show more favoritism to the child they have with you. Sometimes you don't see it but it's easy for you to neglect your older child because of your relationship with your new mate. I see it all the time. Make sure you reiterate to them that it's important to treat the kids equally because you are a package deal. If a man wants to date you and start a family with you, he is also accepting your child as well. That also brings me to the next point I want to touch on ladies and that's please stop putting these men in front of your children.

Chapter 9

Stop Putting Men Ahead of Your Children

Ladies, please stop putting men ahead of your kids. I know some of you are reading this saying to yourself, "My kids come first, he's not talking about me." That may very well be true but don't act like you all don't know the ones who stay in the club Friday, Saturday, and Sunday and then goin' up for two dollar Tuesday and slow it down for thirsty Thursday. She has a new boo every Monday for MCM and her mother damn near raising her kids, oh and don't let me forget she buys man man all the new Jays so she thinks she is doin' something all the while man man is in 4th grade and still can't read and he stutters. I'm not saying don't go out and have fun every now and then but your child should be your first turn up. I'm not tryna' tear you all down when I'm talkin' about this stuff but if you knew better you would do better.

All you beautiful ladies out there are raising our future leaders but it has to start with you. If you meet a man and he never asked about your children or when he invites you out, he does not involve your child, let him go because his only intentions are you and tryna' hit that.

Chapter 10

Trap Queen

I'm just going to come right out and say it- if your man is sellin' drugs out of your house while you have kids that lay their heads there, he does not give a shit about you! I know you want to hold it down and be his ride or die but if you got kids you got more things to worry about than being his trap queen, sweetheart. Having that type of relationship is dangerous around children. Think about this, what is the impact on a child waking up to her mother and her mother's boyfriend's blood and guts splattered all over the house because of a drug deal gone bad. It happens every day. What makes you different? Be with someone who wants to move you away from low level thinking. Let that trap queen mentality go, it's not worth losing your children because in the end men come and go but your children will always be your children. Lame is the new loyal, ladies, I promise. I know y'all love the chase and the drama with other women, the fast life, the bottle poppin', the card crackin, but that only lasts so long. Try seeing what it feels like when a man cares for you more than life itself, hell more than social media -- now that's real love these days.

Chapter 11

Treat Your Sons or Daughters Like Kings and Queens

I wanted to touch base with you on something else that has been bothering me lately. Ladies, please stop yelling at your sons and daughters so much, cursing them out for every little thing. I know you hate his father and he or she is starting to look just like "his sorry ass" but that's not their fault, you chose to lay with their fathers and make a love child or a one-night stand child. Either way it goes, you did it and it's done. Give your babies a hug, tell them you love them every day because even I used to hear my mom say things like, "Sit yo ass down somewhere lookin' just like yo dumbass daddy." As a kid you don't understand what any of that means. Most of the time because of your hate for your child's father you take it out on your kids, and sons get the majority of the resentment. You may not realize you're doing it but unknowingly you are. I remember being kicked out of the house because I looked just like my dad. Lift your sons up, ladies, treat them like kings so that way when he finds the woman for him he will treat them with the same love and respect you showered upon him when he was growing up, hopefully that is. I know it's tough and stressful raising a kid or kids by yourself but you just have to be strong. Ladies, you're queens, you were made for this.

Chapter 12

Abusive Relationships in Front of the Kids

Ladies, I mean this with all my heart, if a man can

put his hands on you, period, or even worse in the

presence of a child, you leave his ass ASAP! He has

no respect for you or women for that matter. I don't

care how much money he has or how many of your

bills he pays it's not worth you and your children's

safety, ladies. I know he says he loves you and it

will never happen again but that's just something I

wouldn't chance, especially with kids in the home.

Growing up this is something I witnessed firsthand.

It was a very traumatizing experience for me being

a child seeing your mother being beat or you sitting

there helpless feeling as if somehow this is your

fault and you could have stopped it. Seeing that as a child can be so confusing, ladies, when I was in middle school and high school, I thought that type of behavior was ok and I had the right to put my hands on my girl because that's what people do when they're in love, right? No! I didn't know any better, and those two years were some of the toughest years of my life. Ladies, I know it's hard to leave but sometimes you have to do what you have to do. If you have to run away to a shelter, do it! No man is worth you not being able to see your kids grow up; sweetheart, no love is worth that. Abuse doesn't always have to be physical, it can be verbal and mental as well. When you're having a heated argument with your boyfriend and he's disrespecting you, calling you out of your name, let me tell you something, those walls are thin. Kids can hear the arguing and it's scary. Believe me I know. I had many sleepless and tearful nights.

I feel a man and woman should never argue in front of the kids. More importantly, a man should never disrespect a woman in front of her kids, because children will begin to resent you for allowing that type of behavior to go on and often causing children to go into a shell resenting not only him but you as well. Sometimes I know fear may play a factor in your decision not to leave, these type of men will threaten your life, the kids' lives, and your family's life but if this is something you're experiencing be strong. At the end of the day no matter how crazy you think he may be, that crazy man doesn't want to go to jail, I can promise you that. No matter how much he threatens you, if he kills you your children grow up without a mother and he's going to jail for life. No man wants to lose their freedom, so never be afraid to call the police on a punk ass man who feels the need to harm you or your children. Father of your children or not, I DO NOT CARE! Worst thing a man can do is put his hands on you beautiful precious queens because that's exactly what you ladies are.

Chapter 13

Switchin' Teams/The "Modern Family"

Switching teams in front of your child, now let's not act slow, you ladies know what switching teams means, but for those of you who don't, it means dating the same sex or becoming a lesbian. Before I go into this topic, I just want to let you ladies know I understand this is a sensitive topic and I do not mean to offend anyone but I believe this topic has to be acknowledged and recognized. Now I don't have any problems with same sex dating, believe me I watch it all the time on the internet, if you know what I mean, just kidding. First off, I do not have any problems with gay and lesbian relationships, who you date is your business and what you do in your home is your business. Like Jay-Z said, "What you eat don't make me shit." So here's the issue I have with the gay/lesbian relationships in front of the children, *you're confusing the child*! No ifs, and or buts about it. Let me explain, if I had a child and my child's mother and I are no longer together and she goes out and gets a girlfriend that's perfectly fine, that's her business. The problem I have with that situation is, my child is seeing this behavior. It's already confusing enough for kids these days growing up, so when that kid sees his mom kissing and hugging a woman or a woman who resembles a man, it could raise a lot of questions.

It's like I wouldn't have an issue if my son/daughter were to be gay, my concern is an innocent child not knowing what's going on between the two of you and being exposed to that type of lifestyle. He or she may grow up thinking that these types of relationships are normal, and let's keep it real, since that is what this book is all about, same sex relationships are not normal. If they were then two women would be able to conceive a child without the help of male sperm, but that's neither here nor there right now. Kids are very impressionable. Say if I had a six-year old daughter and she gets invited to a play date or sleepover and because she often sees her mother kiss her "friend" she decides she is going to kiss her friend, now what? How do I explain to her that girls don't kiss girls or boys don't kiss boys, when she sees her mom doing it? She thinks that type of behavior is "normal." How do I handle that? How do I tell her that although you see your mom kissing her "friend" you're not supposed to kiss girls or boys don't kiss boys?

Again I want to reiterate I do not have a problem with gay/lesbian relationships. But raising a child in that type of situation can be very confusing for him or her. I was talking to a good friend of mine the other day and she and I were having a discussion about this topic. She mentioned to me that she knows some same sex couples that are raising children and she says that those children are being brought up just fine with lots of love. She did mention that one of the couples paints their four-year old son's fingernails but other than that everything seemed normal. Really? That's a red flag for me already. Those are things that just should not be happening because it's not the choice of the child.

Love is love. However, when you switch sides for a temporary thrill or as a means to address an emotional issue its concerning. There is a difference between a short term "switch" and a child being born into that situation. When the mother or father makes the decision to start dating the same sex it's exposing the children to something new. You have to carefully explain what's going on to the child and you have to be straight forward about the role the new mommy or daddy will play in the life of the child. I'll just save the rest of this for the next book because we have a lot to discuss. I will leave you with this note, ladies, give your sons or daughters a fair chance at life, don't expose them to an alternative lifestyle at such a tender and impressionable age because your hurt. For my fellas out there, please step up and be fathers because these lesbians who look and dress like men are raising

your children and taking 'usies' with them for IG.

In Closing

Ladies, when I started writing this it began as me venting. As I began to get into it my views changed and I decided I wanted to help my ladies out. While doing so I had to be honest even if it meant stepping on some toes, but nobody's perfect. We all make mistakes but we learn from them. I hope I was able to reach every one of you because you too have opened my eyes to your situations as well. Being a single mother isn't easy and I have a whole new-found respect for you all. In the words of the late great Tupac Shakur, "I finally understand. It ain't easy for a woman tryna' raise a man; you're appreciated." I hope you enjoyed it,

because there is more where this came from.